The Purple Veil

Kerry Cole

The Creative Journey of The Purple Veil

Back in the mid 90s, Kerry Cole wrote the poem
The Purple Veil and immediately set about presenting it as a stage show.
Employing the choreographic skills of Paula Hocking
it fast became a well-received amateur production.

Envisioned to make the message more widely available,
Kerry teamed up with graphic artist, Billy (David Bill)
with the view of producing each line of the poem as an oil painting.

Enjoying a close working relationship,
Kerry directed the images whilst Billy photographed the
models and painted the pictures.

After six years of detailed planning, consultation and
painting, twelve powerful images have emerged capturing the
heart of the message Kerry is passionate to share.

Her authorship has expanded the poem into a text of great sensitivity
and intimacy which draws the reader into a deep, personal journey.

Contents

The Purple Veil

Take me beyond The Purple Veil into the field of innocence.

There we can run in purity untainted by the crimson stain

The purple fabric allures the eye outstanding in its garishness

Its heady scent has drugged those sleeping underneath its spell.

Awake, awake from slumbers deep

And images of naked hope

For it stirs desire, arouses passion,

But never fulfills body, soul and spirit.

Emotions still scream out for healing.

The brave and courageous pioneer beyond Eros's thicket strong

Daring to believe that there might be

A better way of intimacy.

Kerry Cole 1996

Invitation

Are you up for an adventure?

The pages that lie ahead are an invitation to embark on
a bold and engaging journey.

You will be faced with the challenge of combating the
enslaving power of The Purple Veil.

I must warn you, very few break through it.

The reason The Purple Veil is so explosive is that it
represents the hope we all invest in human relationships
to give us fulfilment, identity and intimacy.

If you have the courage to enter, you will stumble across
many prisoners held captive by the fantasy that a man or
a woman can love them in the way they need to be loved.
Please respect them.
The attraction to The Veil is overwhelmingly powerful for
many a poor traveller.
If you struggle with knowing your true value,
you can easily sell yourself cheaply and become quickly ensnared.

I know this to be true because I had to pass through
The Veil myself and I nearly didn't make it.

Preface

Have you ever gone looking for love?

Have you longed for a relationship to bring you fulfilment?

Maybe you have given your heart away to someone.

Do you have a deep hunger that has led you to become entangled and captivated in some kind of romantic fantasy?

Then you just might find yourself somewhere in these pages.

If you are a seeker I wrote this book for you in the hope that it will help to light your path.

For if you seek you will find, when you seek with all your heart.

Search for the light and then let the light search you.

'Take me beyond The Purple Veil into the field of innocence'

The plea of two young people

Arrayed in white

Shoulder to shoulder

Fighting together

Representing a generation

Strong, determined, over-comers

Pressing forward, travailing, breaking through...

the intense, saturated, impregnated, headiness of The Veil

The trap, the snare

Bewitching, alluring, claiming

Demanding...

their purity - their innocence -

their hope of something better

Something worth fighting for

A return to innocence

A return to Eden

The girl raising her battle scarred shield over her precious heart

The boy lifting the blazing light of truth into the face of darkness, dispelling it, causing it to flee

Taking up the sword together - believing for a pure heart - stepping into the pool of light

Standing in the perfect freedom of their destiny.

'There we can run in purity untainted by the crimson stain'

Two children should be free

to run in the fields with the wind in their hair

and joy tumbling out of their hearts...

Innocence

15

Innocence -

stolen by dark, twisted, entangling hands,

evilly grasping,

coiling around them

Hands that should protect

Eyes that should watch over them for good

Adults

Mentors

Guides

Wise ones

People to look up to

People to trust

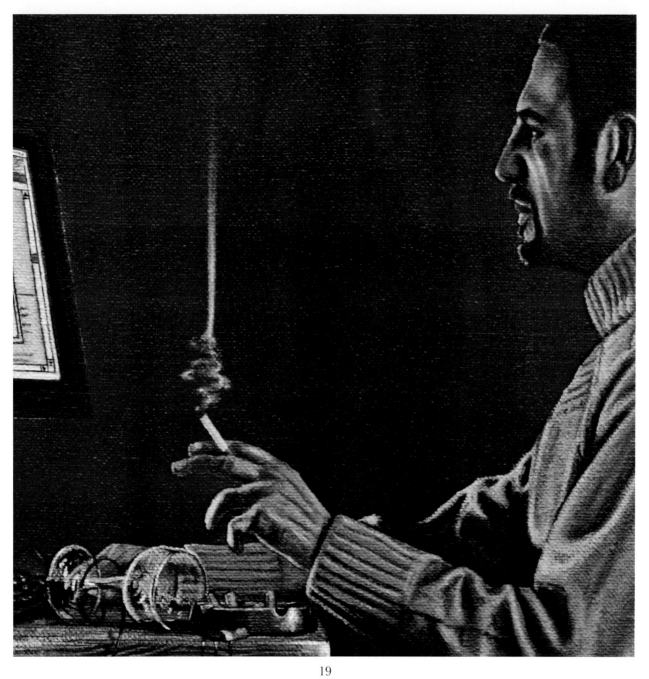

Instead

Exploitation... Corruption... Violation...

Neglect... Lies... Deceit... Betrayal... False love

'Your carelessness is staining my soul,

It is pouring out over my heart.

My tender vulnerability has been spoilt and defiled.

You are hard, oblivious, completely self-centred, reckless in your pursuit of pleasure.

As my body grows older, I may appear normal but my innermost being will carry the cost of this desecration.

You pay quickly with your credit card whilst I have been forced to pay long-term with my life.'

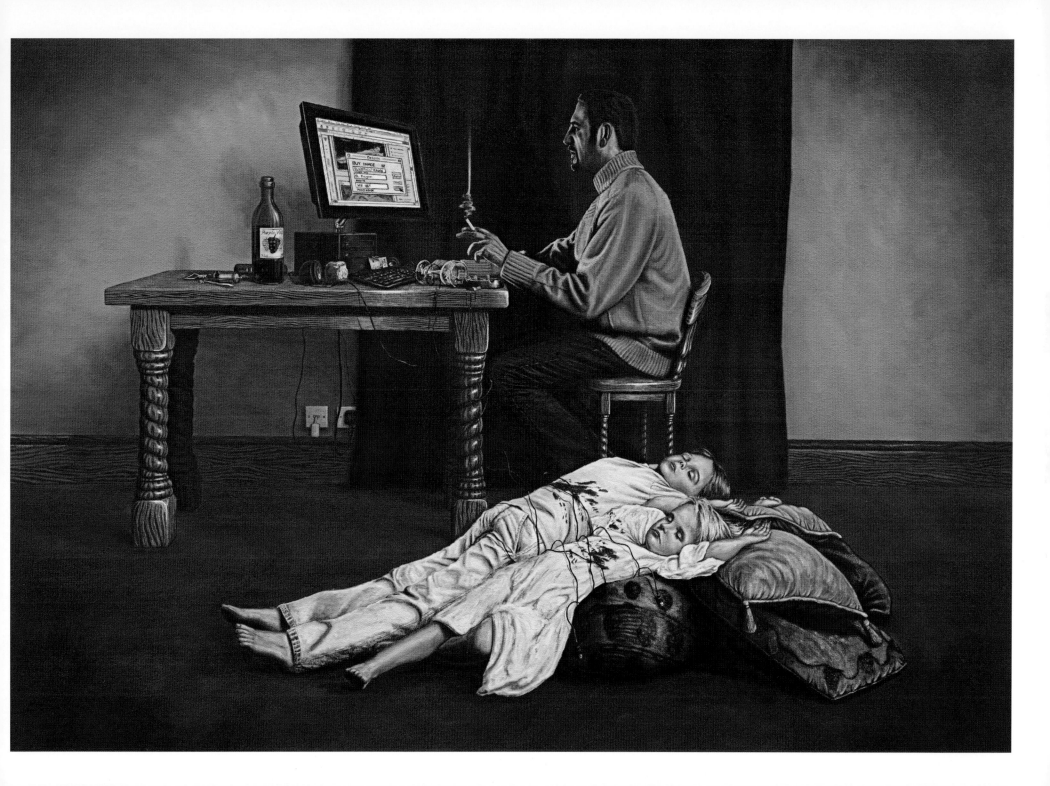

'The purple fabric allures the eye outstanding in its garishness'

A magnetic vision hangs against a disturbed sky

The purple fabric billowing in its hypnotic array

A flamboyant exhibition set on the horizon

Powerfully beckoning, pulling, drawing, enticing, controlling, dominating

Wrestling to overcome my will

Its excessive attractiveness boastfully flaunts - irresistibly alluring, demanding my attention

Calling to my hunger

Crying out to my emptiness

Offering rest

Sanctuary

Hustling me to wrap my broken emotions in its sensuality.

Don't attempt to wake me.

I have fallen asleep here for a reason

Because of a famine

An agonizing emptiness.

In my deep hunger for intimacy this abode with its spectres has filled me

It has satisfied me, crept into my soul and overwhelmed me

I have embraced it and love the relief it provides from my intense loneliness

I can hibernate from my winter of bitter feelings

I am enchanted by this place

For here my imagination is unrestricted by reality

The fantasy of love is drug enough

Intoxicated, I grasp at any person who can embody the phantom

Forcing a real face into my dream -

I worship them

I pull them to me desiring to hold on to them forever

No, don't attempt to wake me; I will rest here sedated in the limbo of denial

This will suffice

It covers the pain

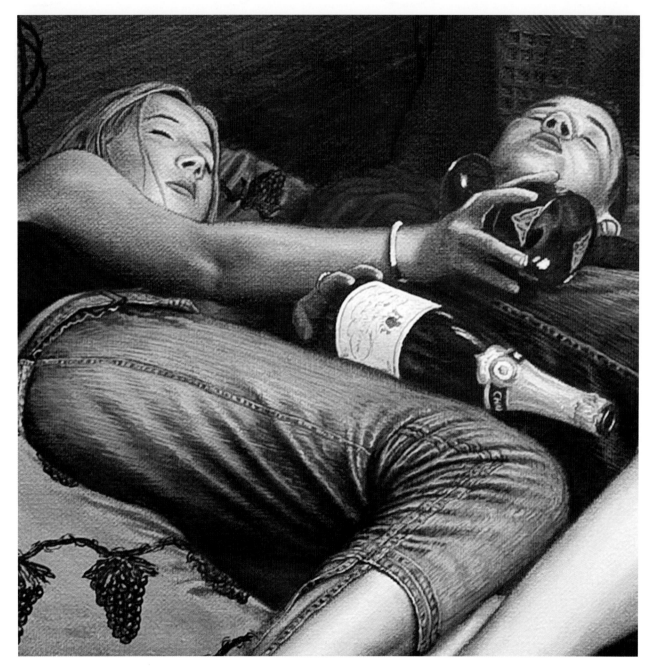

Inside The Purple Veil multitudes lie asleep in an illusion

The whisper of true love calls to the depths -

'If only you would dare to believe that there is a love that is real and true -

you could awake from the counterfeit and flee from this mesmerizing, compromising place.'

'Awake, awake from slumbers deep'

The morning after...

Her conscience awoke as her eyes beheld the daylight

"Where am I?

Whose bed is this?

Who is he?

What happened last night?

Am I pregnant?

Is this love?

Why does my heart feel so broken?

He doesn't really want ME

He was drunk!

He was attracted to me, to my outer appearance - but I'm more than that - the real me deep inside

He's so gorgeous - but where is his heart?

Where is his mind?

Who occupies his thoughts?

It isn't me!

I just fitted into his world temporarily

Like a morsel at midnight I briefly satisfied his appetite

Maybe I was just a snack - a take-away

If I fall asleep once more I will only have to face this later

I must risk the peril of breaking free from this seducing incarceration."

'And images of naked hope'

I am emotionally unavailable, asleep in a world of naked images

An exposed mirage of paper dolls

A powerful imaginary vision

Phantasm

Feast for my eyes to cram into the windows of my soul

But why does it leave me hard and cold, those who long to relate to me angry and frustrated?

Because it's not a real relationship

It only requires a tiny part of me to engage

I can hide my emotional paralysis behind temporary gratification

Yet...

It's like sand through my fingertips

It's a fantasy; I can't hold it

What initially appears so beautiful, so powerfully attractive,

collapses

Instead of being 'King of the Castle,' I become a slave

Dominated, gripped, fettered to its libertine licentiousness

There is no freedom whilst being held captive in this wanton kingdom

The effect of its fascination spews out upon the hordes in tossing waves of yellow bile

Caustic acid

Vomit

A great sea churning in its chemical pollution and toxic waste; damaging everything it comes into contact with

It burns my feet, the feet that were made to stand in reality

I try to touch you and you crumble

If I kiss your face you will disintegrate

But I can handle you better than a real relationship.

'For it stirs desire, arouses passion'

Often the family are the last to know

Whispers

Lies

Secrets

I thought you were my friend...

Betrayal

Destruction

Divorce

Brokenness

Unfaithfulness

It has ripped my heart

"Why couldn't you be faithful? Why did you leave me?

Why did you walk out on us?

Aren't we worth something?

How could you sell us so cheaply?

We thought you were true. We thought you loved us

What is love anyway?

I never saw it from you

I'm scared of relationships now

Why should I trust anyone any more?

I don't need anybody

I've hardened my heart

I'll never let another person in again

Not into the 'true me'

There's no way

I'm emotionally bankrupt

I can't afford it

You betrayed us

It nearly killed mum. She 'hit the bottle' and we are left alone, shattered

There's been an explosion in what should have been our shelter and we have to sit in the ruins

Stunned

Our hearts silenced

Unable to communicate

Just...

tension... sorrow... anger... grief... frustration

So we argue, scream, swear, yell, slam doors, get drunk,

get high to hide the low -

the devastating low."

43

'But never fulfills body, soul and spirit'

My strong hands reach out to pull you to me. Tenacious hands that should be tenderly enfolding my wife

They extend to you and yet I am repulsed

What have I done?

I have given up everything

I've left all I once held dear -

for what?

For a spirit?

You don't really love me - you just allured me, attracted me, distracted me

I gathered you to me but you turned out to be a blazing fire in my lap

And now the sweet wife of my youth weeps and is left abandoned

My kids cry themselves to sleep...

Devoid of identity, desperately insecure without me there to guide and protect them

They spend their hard earned cash on expensive designer clothes just to roll in the gutters of the city streets - drunk

Because they feel worthless

They bear the scars of my unfaithful betrayal

For what? For lust?

For a casual flirtatious whim?

For the ensnarement of one foolish night?

I thought I was in control

You flattered my ego with your smooth tongue

You enslaved me with your alluring body. In the twilight you looked so exquisite

Your scent made me delirious; but now in the cold light of day, I realise you are just a spirit

A spirit of seduction, a spirit of lust inhabiting the body of a difficult and broken woman

I reach for you... I want to hold you... I ache with the lust

But an apparition is hard and indifferent

You don't really want me

God help me!

Is there anyone who can deliver me?

My family is in pieces, they are destroyed and I can't get out of here

There is no handle!

If I could whisper one message into the hearts of my wife and children

I would say

'Just because I didn't realise your value - doesn't mean you are not valuable.

You stagger under the heavy weight of rejection, trying to relieve the agony in your mind because I threw you away

but you are worth more than I could appreciate.'

'Emotions still scream out for healing'

Totally downcast - I languish in the depths of despair

I feel the fire of hell -

fire that eats away my life

Flames that destroy, consuming all the beautiful things I failed to treasure

This fire in which I have sacrificed my precious family

I entered the enticing temple

Not knowing it would be my soul laid out on the altar

Brazen and triumphant the seductive spirit dragged me into its lair

But it has no regard for me, for lust won't satisfy my hunger

It cannot soothe my soul

As deadly as the black widow spider, it hates me and enslaves me

I am merely a fly bundled into its sticky web whilst it spins a snare around another poor victim

'The brave and courageous pioneer beyond Eros's thicket strong'

A letter

A text message

An email -

could negatively change my destiny

'Meet me in the thicket, brave and courageous pioneer'

A moment's decision!

I was on course, travelling in the right direction

When the dark clouds started to gather and swirl ominously

Suddenly a rush of the purple heady scent

A glimpse of The Veil

A beguiling, captivating voice, provoking me to come off the narrow road

To lower my guard

To drop my sword

To become entangled

I feel the intense strength of the desire

I feel the magnitude of The Purple Veil... Yet...

Another voice cries out within me

Wake up

Run

Fight

Flee

Get out from this barbed and thorny den

Take the lead for a far greater adventure!

'Daring to believe that there might be'

The provocative delights offered within The Purple Veil have failed me

What appeared to be so lush and promising has turned out to be a dark and dangerous kingdom

A treacherous desert of rocky land

The cistern from which I drank so deeply has cracked and run dry

The freshness of my beauty is fading

My lovers have abandoned me and disappeared like the morning mist

It is not a small wound that I am left to bear but a serious, incurable injury

My lips are stained with the greedy consumption of the wine of unrestrained lust

The aroma that once drew me hangs in the air as a foul stench

The lurid candle has burnt out.

I have to do this on my own, make my stand

No one else can accomplish this for me

I hear the call of innocence - I sense the promise of a new day - an unblemished start

A sparkling place with unpolluted air, cleansing, gushing streams, living, healing water

A fountain welling up inside of me, rejuvenating, ethereal, heavenly light, refreshing and pure

I deeply breathe the cool reviving atmosphere

I can know freedom

There is another place beyond the appetite of self

A place of true love

There is a door, a gate, a path, a narrow road that leads to life

and if only a few find it - I will be one of them.

'A better way of intimacy'

I hear someone knocking on the door deep inside of me
The bolt lies heavy across my heart
I wrench it back and permit you access
You enter laughing
You flood the place with light - I'm appalled that you see all the chaos
But you say you don't mind the mess, you've come to help me clear it up
You have brought food and prepare it for us to share
It's better than anything I have tasted before and immediately starts to nourish and heal me
You have the kindest eyes
I feel totally safe in your presence
I can tell you anything
You're not shocked
I feel like you know me; REALLY know me
But that doesn't scare me because I sense you have the power to sort everything out and make it good
You stretch out your arms and tell me you want to take me on a journey
I notice some strange marks on your hands
You reveal that they came from forging the way
I marvel at your endurance
The scars look very deep and painful
I sense you have known extreme affliction and self-denial to open up a way for my rescue
I eagerly make for the door, but you explain that we don't have to leave this place because the expedition is within me
You want to take me beyond The Veil
Having already passed through it you've made it possible
Tearing it in two you've destroyed the snare, quenched the hell fire
....
It's a great venture but where does it lead?
I'm intrigued as you announce that we are entering another kingdom and you have someone really special you want me to meet -
Your father...

63

Instantly the air is filled with many angry voices

Multitudes within The Purple Veil begin to wake up and shout out

"Father? That's a strange word to an orphan."

"I met up with my dad in later life and he spat, 'How could I have messed up your life? I was never there!'"

"Are you talking about that drunken geezer who knocked up my Mum?"

"I never knew my dad; he was killed in the war."

"To get approval from my father I had to perform perfectly."

"I don't know who my father was."

A steady stream of words flow from The Veil as the captives give vent to their disturbed emotions...

"abusive, violent, overbearing, sarcastic, disciplinarian, absent, foul-mouthed,

brutal, weak, dogmatic, tyrannical, emotionally void."

Memories of their fatherless-fathers' behaviour flood out in grief and agitation

Vexations from inner bruises and wounds

I crouch in a little ball feeling ice cold

I am disappointed with my prize

The loneliness conjured up by the word 'father' makes me want to run back into the escapism of The Veil

I have a strong urge to comfort myself with its tactile cloth

Then... I meditate on you

Staring at your lacerated hands

I determine to believe that if your father is anything like you then I am going to like him!

Time passes and you teach me about him

You tell me that you're the spitting image of each other

I am amazed to learn that your father wants to be my father too!

I am about to be introduced to a perfect dad...

A tender revelation of your fatherhood wraps around me like a warm blanket of love enfolding my shivering body

My orphaned spirit dissipates under the spirit of adoption

I'm starting to have hope that I'm not alone in this life

Fear no longer controls me as I see the benefits of belonging to you

In light of your loveliness, my previous idolization of relationships seems pathetic in comparison

I don't have to hide under a mass of disguises because my identity is now found

The fear of other people's opinions of me is broken

You emancipate me from my slavery to rituals

You drive unwelcome, dominating forces out of the essence of me

I breathe easy because I am experiencing a massive liberation from cares and anxiety

Your enthusiasm about my unique gifts motivates me to want to share them

Your affirmation of me empowers me to be humble

Your acceptance of me releases me to be authentic

I find myself as I lose myself in you

....

As I receive restoration, I cry out with immense joy

'In you Father, I find my distinctiveness and character

my security, purpose, destiny, ability to love'

I want you to be the blueprint for how I build relationships

You have such attentive eyes that look out for me

Searching eyes that penetrate my soul

But instead of admonishing me you give me beauty for my ashes

Joy instead of my sorrow

What an exchange!

Suddenly I have a mental flashback to The Veil

It was never all it was made out to be

I had some horrible experiences

I remember certain people who used me when I was in there

Father listens intently to my complaint and leads me down to a free-flowing river

As I cry and forgive them, he gently points out that I have used people too

As they come into my memory, I feel heavy but then he compassionately starts to wash my feet and tells me that I can walk in a new way

All the pent up guilt and shame seems to drain out of me and float away

I am left feeling light-hearted and peaceful

He's such a good dad!

When I ask him how he can forgive me, he tells me it is because of my best friend, the man who had originally come to my house

"He made the way for you darling," he laughs

I look up and a little girl has run through The Veil

She's a lovely child, clothed in a beautiful white dress... I gasp as I notice an ugly stain across her heart

Your strong arms reach out for her, encompassing her, they gather her in

A soft white snow lands gently upon the scarlet blemish

The discolouration is completely covered and then dissolves

Assured of your pure affections for her and secure in your love, she skips off into the daisies and chamomile...

Not to constraint or limitations, nor into a box of rules

but toward extravagant freedom, where the only boundaries are ones of love, governed by rich, deep, heart relationship

....

I glance towards The Veil and marvel to see multitudes breaking through it

I believe that as we walk through life with you, we will be able to declare

'Father, your heart is faithful and true, everything you do is motivated by love... and you would even die for us...

to take us beyond The Purple Veil.'

Kerry Cole was born in the South West of England in Plymouth.

A child of the sixties, she was greatly influenced by the creative blends of music, fashion, art and literature which helped define the popular culture of that extraordinary decade.

She married Chris Cole in 1982 and together they founded the UK media organisation Cross Rhythms.

Living in a house which is nestled into a cliff, Kerry thrives on the sea air of the wild Cornish coast.

Billy (David Bill) got to work on The Purple Veil project with Kerry through a mutual love of Pre-Raphaelite art, especially John Waterhouse. Billy, in his art career, has been thrown out of an aeroplane with the Red Devils, taken down a salt mine, and worked occasionally on terra firma based projects with, among others, Aston Martin Cars, the BBC, Britannia Building Society and numerous motorcycle racers.

Billy is married to Sharon, they have three children, a poochie and five chickens.

Visit our gallery at

www.thepurpleveil.com

1. Overcoming Generation

2. Innocence Plundered

3. Magnetic Array

4. Hypnotic Slumber

5. The Morning After

6. Naked Hope

7. The Betrayal

8. No Way Out

9. Brazen Conquest

10. Dark Thicket

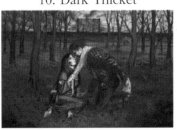

11. Daring to Believe

12. Turning of Hearts